Why this book?

Do you have trouble with sleep? Do yo

- find you cannot drop off to sleep at night
- drop off happily but then wake in the early hours
- toss and turn for most of the night?

Or do you have other problems associated with sleep,
such as:

- restless legs syndrome
- obstructive sleep apnoea
- night cramps?

Perhaps you do a job that means your sleep is disrupted.
Do you:

- have to do shift work
- often suffer from jet lag?

Whatever your problem with your sleep, this book is for
you. Written by a family doctor who has seen every sleep
problem there is in his surgery, *First steps through Insomnia*
will tell you everything you need to know to achieve your
eight hours of blissful slumber.

First Steps through Insomnia

Dr Simon Atkins

All advice given is for information only and should not be treated as a substitute for qualified medical advice.

Text copyright © 2014 Simon Atkins
This edition copyright © 2014 Lion Hudson

Published by Lion Books
an imprint of
Lion Hudson plc
Wilkinson House, Jordan Hill Road,
Oxford OX2 8DR, England
www.lionhudson.com/lion

ISBN 978 0 7459 5620 6
e-ISBN 978 0 7459 5781 4

First edition 2014

A catalogue record for this book is available from the British Library

Printed and bound in Malta, February 2014, LH28

For my wife Nikki,
for whom sleep is often elusive

Contents

Introduction

Although we can disagree on many things in life – our political views, which sports teams to support, whether there is a God or not, or, most importantly for some, who's the best James Bond – there is one thing that gets unanimous agreement every time: there is absolutely nothing quite like a good night's sleep.

Even the phrase itself – "a good night's sleep" – makes you feel all warm and snuggly inside. And it conjures up all sorts of wonderful images of being engulfed in a comfortable bed where you enjoy eight solid hours of sweet dreams before waking completely refreshed in the morning. Unfortunately, for one in five of us worldwide that ideal situation is itself just a forlorn dream, and a good night's sleep is elusive – something that only happens to other people.

My wife, Nikki, is one of those 20 per cent who suffer from chronic insomnia. Most nights of the week she struggles to drop off to sleep, wakes regularly, and then can't drift off again for hours at a time. I very often wake up to find it's the middle of the night and her spot beside me in the bed is cold and empty because she has popped downstairs for a warm drink and a change of scenery, to relieve the frustrating monotony of lying awake alone.

Once she's awake, of course, her brain kicks in with thoughts of what happened the day before and what needs to be done in the morning, both for herself and our three boys. She then finds herself repeatedly checking the LED clock on the bedside cabinet, which only serves to remind her of how long she's been awake battling these thoughts.

And to make matters worse, she has to lie next to a husband who from time to time (more often than not if you believe her accounts) snores, talks in his sleep, and grinds his teeth – and sometimes does all three together. Unfortunately, no matter how much she nudges him, he just doesn't wake up and sleeps through most nights like a baby, waking in the morning as if nothing has happened, whereas she can recount tales of next-door neighbours who noisily got in at three, a milkman's chinking bottles at five, and the wretched birdsong of the dawn chorus just before six.

I also see countless patients in my surgery with the same symptoms. Some can't sleep because of the effects of other medical problems, while others, like Nikki, cannot explain why they have this hellish condition.

Fortunately, there are treatments available for insomnia, and over the course of this book we will look at these in turn, to find out how they work and what evidence there is, if any, for their effectiveness. Unfortunately, as you'll see, there are no quick fixes, and the therapies that work best require hard work and determination.

There are a number of other things that can affect sleep too, quite apart from straight insomnia. These include

First Steps through Insomnia

sleep apnoea, night cramps, restless legs, jet lag, and shift work. And we will look at the causes and treatments for all of these as well.

But in the first part of the book we begin by exploring the whole subject of why we go to sleep in the first place and what a normal sleep pattern looks like, followed by a chapter discussing what insomnia really is.

My wife has been helped by many of the treatments covered in this book. If it wasn't for all the noise coming from her husband, she might have had a good night's sleep every night.

1
Why we sleep

Sleep is a biological feature of the lives of all mammals on the planet. Every squirrel, manatee, tiny little shrew, and magnificent elephant will have its necessary share of shut-eye. Birds and fish go to sleep too and there's also evidence that invertebrate species such as bees and scorpions have periods during every twenty-four hours when they are less responsive than usual and seem to have dozed off.

The amount of sleep needed varies wildly between species from the brown bat, which will spend 19.9 hours of every day out for the count, to the giraffe, which naps for just 1.9 hours out of every twenty-four.

For humans, our "normal" sleep duration changes as we get older. As babies, we spend an average of sixteen hours a day asleep (waking only at night to frustrate our parents). We will get around eight hours through most of adulthood, but only five and a half when we reach old age. And, of course, teenagers will try to avoid getting up at all when possible!

Why do we sleep?

Given that sleep seems to have evolved across an enormous range of species, there must be some sort of critical biological need for us to doze off for a few hours every night. But, despite years of research, the jury is still out about what the purpose of sleep actually is. There are, however, a number of well-established theories put forward to explain it.

Evolutionary theory

One of the earliest theories about sleep was that it served as a protective mechanism by keeping animals out of harm's way when it was dark, when they would be more vulnerable to being killed and eaten by something with sharper teeth and claws that they didn't see until it was too late. This is backed up by the fact that animals with few predators tend to sleep longer than those who are regularly on the menu of other creatures.

However, there's an obvious flaw in this theory because the fact that your prey is sound asleep at night, and therefore unaware you are sneaking up on it, no doubt makes late-night dining even more attractive for predators, who will have to do very little work to earn their supper. As sleeping prey, you might as well be presented on a plate with a knife and fork laid out ready beside you.

It's also been suggested that sleep evolved to allow for energy conservation, which makes a little more sense, but the vulnerability issue still persists.

Repair and restoration theory

This theory says that we go to sleep so that our bodies and brains can be restored and revitalized and keep functioning at an optimum, healthy level. It's thought that, as part of this process, tissues are repaired and the brain gets rid of toxic waste products.

To use a computer analogy, it's a bit like sleep allows us to run a disk check, virus scan, and defragmentation of our hard drives.

Information consolidation theory
Proponents of this theory have evidence to suggest that during sleep the brain consolidates information it's taken in the day before in order to prepare for tomorrow. It also gives the brain a chance to make long-term memories more permanently hard-wired.

In conclusion

What's clear from the fact that there are so many theories is that we don't really know why we sleep. It's likely that there's some truth in all of them and that we go to sleep for a number of important reasons.

What happens if we don't have enough sleep?
Although there is obvious argument about *why* we sleep, there is plenty of agreement about what happens if we don't get enough of it. Some of the effects are serious, whereas others are more of an annoyance, affecting our ability to function normally at home or at work.

Serious consequences of lack of sleep
If you suffer from long-term sleep deprivation, you are at increased risk of a number of conditions that can be potentially life-threatening. The big five of these are listed below.

 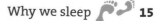

- *Obesity*. If you regularly have poor sleep, you are 30 per cent more likely to become obese than those who sleep well. The culprits here are thought to be two hormones that control our appetite. If you are sleep-deprived, you will have a higher level of ghrelin, which boosts appetite, and low levels of leptin, which makes us feel full after a meal.

- *Diabetes*. Poor sleep affects the way our bodies deal with blood sugar and increases the risk of developing diabetes. Add to this what we have just observed about the affect of insomnia on obesity, which is also a risk factor for diabetes, and the overall risk gets even higher.

- *High blood pressure*. Lack of sleep will raise your blood pressure to persistently high levels, and if you already have hypertension it will push it up further. The reason for this isn't yet clear, though.

- *Heart disease*. A combination of higher blood pressure and raised levels of inflammatory chemicals in the bloodstream of poor sleepers makes damage to blood vessel walls more likely, and this can trigger heart disease. Chronic insomnia also causes a raised pulse level, which is another contributing factor.

- *Depression and anxiety*. Sleep is needed to maintain good mental health, and a long-term lack of it will put you at risk of low mood and nervousness. One research study of 10,000 people found that poor sleepers were five times more likely to suffer from depression than those who slept well.

Other consequences

- *Poor fertility and sex drive.* If you are tired from lack of sleep, there's a good chance that your sex drive will be really low compared with someone who's rested and therefore "raring to go". Reproductive hormone cycles are also upset by insomnia and this can affect your chances of conceiving.

- *Reduced immunity.* Sleep helps keep your immune system ticking over and without it you are likely to pick up every cough and cold that's going around.

- *Greater risk of having accidents.* When you're sleepy in the daytime, concentration is down and you are much more likely to be clumsy and accident-prone. On a more tragic level, all too many people have died as a result of drivers falling asleep at the wheel.

- *Lack of mental sharpness.* Without sleep, there is a good chance that your memory, concentration, and other thought processes will be on a go-slow, affecting your ability to carry out even simple tasks at home and at work.

- *Older-looking skin.* Two more hormones can be affected by insomnia and both have a detrimental effect on the state of your skin. Cortisol levels go up, causing a breakdown in collagen, which keeps the skin supple and stretchy. And levels of growth hormone, which repairs tissues while we sleep, go down. This combination leads to more wrinkles and more rapid aging of your skin.

- *Irritability.* Probably the most minor effect of insomnia in terms of long-term harm to your body, but top of the list when it comes to reasons for upsetting other people.

Counting sheep helps you get to sleep.
In 2002, when psychologists from Oxford University put
this to the test with a group of people who had insomnia,
they found that those who counted sheep actually took
longer to drop off than those who imagined relaxing
situations such as lying on a beach.

In this chapter I've repeatedly used the term "insomnia"
without really explaining what it means. In Chapter 3 we
will look at this in some detail, but first we will discuss
how sleep works.

2

What happens while we're sleeping

Normal sleep architecture

This is the technical phrase used to describe the pattern of a typical night's sleep. It was first discovered by scientists who were measuring people's brain activity using apparatus called an electroencephalogram. This equipment records brainwaves by sticking small electrodes to the scalp. These pick up the electrical signals produced by our brain cells when they communicate with each other, which can then be recorded on a computer.

It was noticed that when we are awake the pattern of activity recorded is very fast and the waves are small, whereas when we fall asleep the pattern changes to become slower, with larger waves. Once we hit deep sleep, the waves become slower and deeper still – these are called delta waves. Finally, the researchers identified a stage of sleep when the pattern again becomes fast and of high frequency, as if the person was awake. This was noted to be associated with rapid movements of the person's eyes and earned the name "rapid eye movement" or REM sleep. The remaining, slower wave sleep is called non-REM sleep or NREM.

(RAPID EYE MOVEMENT)

REM

awake

sleepy

EEG
(WAVE FORMS)

deep

sleep

Stages of sleep

N
R
E
M

- Stage 1: The transition from being awake to dropping off to sleep
- Stage 2: Light sleep as the brainwaves start to slow down
- Stage 3: Deeper sleep, first with a mixture of light sleep brainwaves and delta waves
- Stage 4: All waves are delta waves
- REM sleep

NREM sleep
In the periods of NREM, we breathe more steadily and have a lower heart rate than during REM sleep. Muscles are still active during NREM sleep and this is what often causes us to have violent muscle twitches when we kick out just as we are dropping off. We can dream in these periods of sleep but our dreams will be less vivid than in REM sleep.

REM sleep
During REM sleep, our breathing is faster, our pulse goes up, and our blood pressure rises. Dreams tend to last longer and are much more complex, bizarre, hallucinatory, and delusional. REM sleep is also a time when men have nocturnal erections.

Cycles of sleep
We alternate between these two types of sleep in cycles of REM/NREM that each last for 90–100 minutes and are repeated throughout the night. The illustration below shows the stages of sleep we pass through in each cycle.

As you'll see, during an average night's sleep we will go through four or five of these cycles, with the proportion of REM/NREM sleep in each cycle changing through the night, higher levels of REM sleep appearing as the night goes on. Overall, though, 75 per cent of our sleep is NREM.

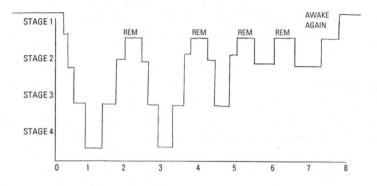

The sleep–wake cycle

The section above has explained the processes involved in sleep itself. We now need to look at how the brain also controls our ability to switch between sleep and wakefulness, so that we have the correct amounts of each. This is imaginatively called the sleep–wake cycle.

The brain has two regulatory mechanisms which act alongside each other to control this cycle. One of these is called our circadian system; the other, which works rather like an oscillating hourglass (see below), keeps tabs on how long we have been awake.

Circadian system

This system, sometimes referred to as our body clock, is centred in a part of the brain called the hypothalamus, specifically in the suprachiasmatic nucleus. Here, a small group of nerve cells are responsible for generating a twenty-four-hour rhythm in the body.

These cells are stimulated by messages from your eyes, which allow them to respond to the different levels of light and dark around you, depending on what time of day or night it is. This then sets the pattern for control of various hormone levels, body temperature, pulse, and blood pressure. One of these hormones is melatonin, which is released by the pineal gland in the brain in response to dropping light levels to directly trigger sleepiness.

Hourglass oscillator

With this system, which carries on in a continual rhythm, the chances of falling asleep increase the longer you have been awake and vice versa. It's probably easier to visualize using the diagram below.

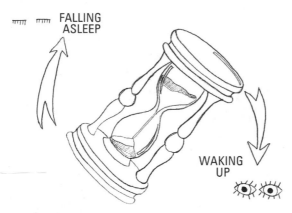

FALLING ASLEEP

WAKING UP

These two systems have to work together to produce good sleep at night and alertness in the day. If one is disrupted, however, there will be a mismatch and the quality of sleep will be significantly affected. Most commonly, it is the body clock that is messed up, and we will see the effect of this in later chapters.

The two systems can also work slightly differently in different people, which accounts for why some people – often called "larks" – are bright as a button in the morning and ready for action, but have no energy to stay up late at night; whereas others – "owls" – take a while to get going when they wake up but are always ready for a late-night party and are usually the last ones standing.

Now that we have looked at normal sleep, we will begin in the next chapter to look at insomnia.

3
What is insomnia?

If we are going to get to grips with the problem of insomnia, we first need to make sure of what we mean by the word, so that we know we are talking about the same thing. We all have different tolerance levels for symptoms and there is such a wide range of what is "normal" in human experience that one person's chronic insomnia may simply be another's bad night. For some, getting six hours' sleep may be a luxury, so if someone else complains that they can never drop off for eight hours straight, the six-hour person will wonder what all the fuss is about.

I see this disparity regarding symptoms in my surgery all the time. Bowel habit is another good example. Some people think constipation refers to having rock-hard poo instead of soft motions. Others, who are much nearer the mark, understand it to be a reduction in frequency of going to the toilet. But there's more possible confusion here. The normal range for frequency of passing a stool (ridiculous medical language) is anything from three times each day to once every three days. So a three-a-day woman might begin to worry she's constipated if she starts only having to go once every twenty-four hours, whereas a once-every-three-days man probably won't consider consulting until he hasn't had a turn-out for a week or so.

So, not only is a factual definition of a medical condition important, but so also is knowledge of the normal range and an individual's usual pattern. We're looking for changes from normal for the individual concerned, rather than from a perceived gold standard description: less than your usual frequency, not less than the average.

Insomnia

If we return from problems on the toilet to troubles with sleeping in bed, then there are a number of different definitions to consider when we talk about insomnia.

Insomnia itself is defined as difficulty in getting to sleep, difficulty staying asleep, early wakening, or non-refreshing sleep despite having adequate time and opportunity to sleep. But it can further be categorized as short- or long-term, primary or secondary. And to complicate things further, some people have early insomnia where they only have trouble getting off to sleep, whereas others have no problems drifting off as soon as their head hits the pillow, but will wake extremely early and not get off again. For some unfortunates, it's a combination of these two problems.

Primary insomnia

Primary insomnia affects around 25 per cent of all insomnia sufferers. It is defined as insomnia that occurs despite there being no other medical, psychological, or environmental triggers. It must last for at least one month to fit the diagnosis and may be a problem of either getting to sleep or staying asleep.

What causes it?

Specialists working in the area of insomnia have identified two main causes. The first of these is "sleep misperception". This means that although you think you're not getting much sleep and are awake for half the night, you are in fact sleeping like a baby and getting all the rest you need. The second cause, termed "idiopathic insomnia", seems to happen in people whose brains don't switch off at night due to a problem with the sleep–wake cycle (see Chapter 2). This problem is called "hyper-arousal", but for sufferers it is certainly not arousing in a good way.

Misperception

When researchers Allison Harvey and Nicole Tang published a paper on this in 2012, they identified thirteen possible explanations for the way in which insomnia sufferers may misperceive their sleep. Below is a selection of those.

- As we start to drift off, there is period when we have an altered level of both consciousness and memory. Because of this combination, watching the clock during the night gives us an inaccurate picture of the length of time we have been asleep.

- People can vary in the way they perceive the onset of sleep, so the time from lights out to dropping off is overestimated.

- Ongoing psychological stress can make us magnify other distressing issues in our lives, such as lack of sleep.
- We are not able to estimate time accurately.
- Worry when we are awake in the night gives us an exaggerated idea of how long we are awake.
- Sufferers think their frequent transient periods of wakefulness actually mean they are awake most of the night, whereas in fact sleep tests show they are not.

Hyper-arousal

This is the number-one cause of primary insomnia and means that, instead of settling down for the night, the brain of a sufferer seems to want to get going again. In technical parlance, their brain has heightened sensory, information, and memory processing at night. If this is you, then you will classically:

- be more aware of the noise and/or temperature of your surroundings
- ruminate on the problems of the past day or have to plan for the next one
- be very aware of how a bad night's sleep will affect you the next day
- have great difficulty getting to sleep every night.

None of this will be helped by a whole set of physical differences that scientists have found between people with primary insomnia and those who effortlessly enjoy a good night's sleep. These include:

- increased heart rate
- lower levels of the sleep hormone melatonin
- slightly raised body temperature
- higher level of metabolism in the brain suggesting it's more active in insomniacs.

Secondary insomnia

This is by far the most common form of the condition, accounting for the remaining 75 per cent of cases of insomnia. The symptoms are exactly the same as in primary insomnia but the causes are extremely wide-ranging. Secondary insomnia can therefore be thought of as a side effect of another situation or condition. Some of the main culprits are:

- painful conditions: arthritis, headache disorders (such as migraine or tension headache), dental pain, backache
- conditions that affect breathing: asthma, chronic bronchitis and emphysema, heart failure
- hormonal fluctuations: an overactive thyroid condition (hyperthyroidism), menopausal hot flushes, menstruation and premenstrual syndrome, pregnancy
- gastrointestinal disorders: heartburn, indigestion, reflux, hiatus hernia
- mental health problems: depression, anxiety, bipolar disorder, dementia
- other sleep disorders: restless legs syndrome, night cramps, sleep apnoea, jet lag, working odd shift patterns
- stimulants: alcohol, nicotine, caffeine

- side effects of medicines for: blood pressure (such as alpha and beta blockers), high cholesterol (statins), depression (SSRIs such as Prozac), prostate symptoms (Flomax), and chronic lung diseases (salbutamol inhalers and prednisolone tablets).

And last, but by no means least...

- your partner: many people struggle to get a good night's sleep because their other half snores, talks in their sleep, grinds their teeth loudly, or repeatedly gets up to go to the toilet.

With a list this long, all of us are going to suffer from at least some of these things at some point, and so it's a miracle that anyone gets any sleep at all. But what it also means is that by treating any obvious triggers like those listed above, many people can have their insomnia dealt with easily.

Duration of insomnia

Insomnia can also be classified according to how long the problem lasts:

- transient insomnia: insomnia that lasts for only a few days
- short-term insomnia: lasts for no more than three weeks
- long-term (or chronic) insomnia: lasts for more than one month.

Both primary and secondary insomnia can be transient, short-term, or long-term.

This brief discussion of definitions should ensure that we are talking about the same problem when we talk about insomnia. And although it can mean just a few bad nights that will make the best of us feel grouchy, the rest of this book will be concerned with longer-term, chronic insomnia, the type that can really make us feel unwell and unfit to function normally.

Symptoms of insomnia

- Lying awake for a long time in bed every night before dropping off to sleep.
- Waking up frequently during the middle of the night.
- Waking up early every morning and not being able to get back to sleep again.
- A combination of all three of the above.
- Feeling tired and not refreshed by sleep.

In the next chapter, we will take a look at the long list of disabling consequences that chronic insomnia can lead to.

Mythbuster

Insomnia is a purely psychological problem.
Unfortunately, although it can be triggered by worries and more serious mental health problems, poor sleep is much more commonly caused by a wide range of physical problems such as chronic pain from arthritis or breathing difficulties.

4

Your appointment with the doctor

If you are beginning to suffer because of your insomnia, it is certainly worth making an appointment with your family doctor to see if they can help get to the bottom of why you are having trouble sleeping. They might even have some treatments up their sleeves to alleviate matters.

They will have a number of questions to ask you to help rule in or out various diagnoses, and they will want to go through your medication list and get a handle on your eating, drinking, and smoking habits. Be honest with them, because they can't help you if you give them false information, so if you do smoke in bed or have a skinful of booze every evening, tell them. Likewise, you might want to write down notes on your sleep pattern, or even keep a diary (see below), so that you can get across what's happening to you in the most complete way possible.

Questions about your sleep pattern

Simply telling your doctor that you are an insomniac who wants fixing is not enough information for them to go on, so be ready for them to ask you a long list of specifics. They will need to know:

- what time you put the lights out
- how long it roughly takes for you to drop off
- how long it is before you first wake up in the night
- how many times you wake up altogether
- how long you remain awake each time
- at what time you finally wake in the morning
- whether you sleep during the daytime
- what time you get out of bed in the morning
- whether you do shift work.

The answers to these questions will allow the doctor to calculate the percentage of time you are actually asleep between turning off the light at night and getting up in the morning. They will also enquire about whether you snore and whether anyone has ever said you've stopped breathing while you are asleep.

Questions about your lifestyle

A number of lifestyle factors are important in helping or hindering sleep. These include:

- whether you smoke cigarettes
- your daily alcohol intake
- how much caffeine you drink in tea or coffee and when you drink it

- your use of street drugs
- the size and timing of your evening meal
- the amount of exercise you get each day
- what you do in bed. Yes, they will ask about the obvious (because that's allowed!), but, more importantly, they will want to know about your habits regarding use of computers, watching television, and whether you eat and drink in bed.

Questions about your mental health

A number of mental health issues – from stress in your workplace or a recent bereavement, to full-on bipolar disorder – can have a significant impact on your ability to get off to sleep and stay unconscious.

The doctor will want to ask about symptoms of stress, anxiety, and depression, and they may ask you to fill out a questionnaire designed to help diagnose these problems.

Questions about your general health

If you're seeing a doctor you know well, which is always best for continuity of care, they will know the details of your medical history and types of medicine you have been prescribed. But if you are new to them, they will specifically ask about whether you have any painful conditions and for details of pills you are prescribed or buy from the pharmacy, to help these other conditions.

They will also want to know if you ever sleepwalk, have restless legs in bed at night, or are woken by nightmares.

What's next?

Once they have taken a detailed medical and sleeping

history from you, they may carry out a targeted physical examination if anything you've said suggests you may have an undiagnosed problem upsetting your sleep. An example here might be prostate gland trouble in a man who is kept awake by repeatedly having to get up to pass urine every night.

Blood and urine tests may also be suggested, as certain conditions that can be picked up with these tests, such as thyroid gland dysfunction, can affect sleep. And finally the doctor may well also ask you to fill in a detailed diary over one to two weeks to return to them.

Once they have been able to put all this information together, they will then review it and discuss treatment options with you.

What might they suggest?

If there is an obvious trigger for your poor sleep – meaning you have secondary insomnia – then your doctor will want to treat the cause rather than the symptom, in the hope that this will improve your sleep. This might be better pain relief for arthritis at night-time, or medication or psychotherapy for underlying depression.

If it's thought that the problem is primary insomnia, then treatment will focus on sorting out your sleep directly. In the next few chapters we will go through the different types of prescription medicines, psychotherapies, and alternative therapies that are available to treat this type of insomnia, focusing on the benefits and side effects of each.

First, though, we will look at tried and tested self-help methods that may sort out the problem without you having to resort to any more specialized treatments, or waste money on ineffective over-the-counter remedies. These methods focus on improving what's called your "sleep hygiene". Chances are you have some very unhygienic habits in the bedroom.

Mythbuster

Alcohol can help you get a good night's sleep.
Many people will have an alcoholic "nightcap" before bed to help them get to sleep. Often this is a drop of whisky but it might be a beer or two, or a couple of glasses of wine or port. Although the sedative effect of alcohol will indeed get you off to sleep OK, as the alcohol is metabolized in your body your sleep will become lighter, making you more likely to have broken sleep and to wake up unrefreshed by the experience.

5
Sleep hygiene

This odd-sounding term has nothing whatsoever to do with scrubbing behind your ears, cleaning under your fingernails, or washing your hands when you've been to the toilet – although these are all very important in their own right (especially the last one!). Sleep hygiene is all about the way in which you establish good daytime and night-time routines and a cosy bedroom environment that are conducive to getting a good night's sleep. And the good news is that following these simple do's and don'ts can improve poor sleep no end.

Do

- Ideally, go to bed and get up in the morning at the same time each day, as this will get your body into a good rhythm.
- Take regular exercise each day, in the morning if possible. Around thirty minutes per day of doing

anything that puts your pulse up is ideal. This can include taking the dog out, using stairs instead of the lift, and getting off the bus or train one or two stops earlier and walking the rest of your journey. It need not mean joining a gym, going swimming, or taking up jogging – although if you have a penchant for doing things that involve wearing Lycra, all of those are obviously good too.

- Make sure you have plenty of exposure to natural outdoor light, or bright lights indoors in the winter, especially in the late afternoon. This again helps to establish your body's day–night rhythms.

- Keep the temperature in your bedroom just right and certainly neither too hot so you're fidgety and have to keep throwing off the covers, nor too cold so that you have to wear ten layers of clothing, a woolly hat, and socks.

- Use your bed only for sleep and sex. You will never get either if you eat your tea in it, are forever watching films or TV, or use it to complete office work. (And you're unlikely to have the latter wrapped up in your woolly hat and socks, which is another important reason to have a comfortable room temperature.)

- Keep the bedroom dark enough to allow you to drop off to sleep, with curtains closed and blackout blinds in summer if needed.

- Make sure the bedroom is quiet and therefore has a restful ambience. If you live on a busy street, sleep at the back of your house or flat if possible. Get some earplugs if needed to avoid being woken by noise and perhaps block out the sound of your other half snoring.

- Use relaxation exercises just before going to sleep or listen to a relaxation tape (or podcast).

- Try relaxing your muscles and mind by taking a warm bath or having a massage. Scented candles and aromatic oils may help as long as you don't leave the candles alight and risk setting fire to your bedroom. Have a warm, milky drink before you hit the sack.

Don't

- Never exercise just before going to bed as you'll be sweaty and full of adrenaline and endorphins.

- Don't fall victim to "electronic insomnia" (e-somnia?) by playing video games, surfing the net, responding to emails, or watching an adrenaline-pumping TV show or movie just before bed. They will all make it very difficult for you to switch off afterwards.

- Don't sit down just before bed to have an important discussion or phone call with a loved one, particularly if it's about a contentious issue and likely to lead to a row.

- Avoid caffeine after your evening meal – so no coffee, tea, or chocolate bars unless they are explicitly labelled decaff.

- Don't drink alcohol in the evening or use alcohol to sleep. It will cause you to wake early and, if you've drunk a little too much, will have you going to the toilet through the night and waking with a hangover.

- Don't smoke before going to bed, or in bed. Nicotine is a stimulant and will keep you awake, and cigarettes, like scented candles, are a fire risk.

- Never watch television in bed. It will kill sleep and passion, and make you break the golden rule above about only using your bed for sleep and sex.

- Don't go to bed too hungry or too full. Neither indigestion nor hunger pangs are relaxation aids.

- Never take another person's sleeping pills, or any of their other pills for that matter.

- Never take daytime naps or doze off in front of the TV in the evening as this will seriously mess with your body clock.

- Don't try to force yourself to go to sleep. This only makes you more alert, as your thoughts keep reminding you that you are still not asleep.

- Don't lie in bed awake for more than twenty to thirty minutes, getting ever more frustrated about your lack of sleep. Get up, go to a different room, and read or do a quiet activity for a bit, or have a milky drink and then return to bed.

- Don't have a fluorescent bedside clock reminding you what the time is throughout the night. Turn it to face away from you or put it under the bed. *And leave it alone!* A constant reminder of how little you've slept will not help your brain switch off and let you sleep.

6

Drug treatments for insomnia

Medicine has a number of tricks up its sleeve to help treat insomnia. In this chapter we will deal with drugs that have been specifically designed to help users to get off to sleep and some others which, although not made with insomnia treatment in mind, can help sleep as a by-product of their other purposes.

The history of sleeping tablets

Given that insomnia is such a common problem, it's not surprising that our ancestors tried developing medicines for it way back in the time of the pharaohs. Both the Egyptians and the Greeks are thought to have used opium as a treatment for sleep problems, and the Romans used a number of herbal treatments including mandrake. (The correct dosage of this last one is crucial – too much and you won't wake up again.)

It wasn't until the nineteenth century, though, that medicines were developed that could be manufactured for large numbers of people. In the 1800s, the main drug used was chloral hydrate, which induces sleep by depressing the functions of the central nervous system. Used by criminals as "knock-out drops" (the infamous Mickey Finn), it was taken for medicinal purposes by a number of well-known figures such as Friedrich Nietzsche and Marilyn Monroe.

In the early twentieth century, a new group of medicines called barbiturates became the drug of choice for sleeping problems. They not only helped with getting people off to sleep but also helped with stress, anxiety, and agitation. Unfortunately, this group of drugs is extremely addictive and so became widely abused. Barbiturates also carry a high risk of death by overdose, which became increasingly common when their users took them with alcohol, and they are therefore rarely used now in medicine.

The other major drug group for sleep, which became available in the last century, were the benzodiazepines and it's this group of drugs that really took off and cornered the market. Drugs like temazepam, nitrazepam, and diazepam (perhaps better known as restoril, mogadon, and valium respectively) came into heavy use not only for insomnia but for psychiatric conditions such as anxiety, too. They are still in widespread use now, so we will look at them next in more detail.

Finally, there are the most recently manufactured insomnia medicines, which are called Z-drugs, as their names, such as zopiclone and zolpidem, all begin with that letter.

Benzodiazepines

Since the 1960s this group of drugs has been the most commonly prescribed type of medicine for insomnia, as well as being used to treat anxiety and panic attacks. Benzodiazepines come in either short- or long-acting forms – the shorter-acting sort being used to help sleep, as they wear off by morning, and the longer-acting forms being used to help manage anxiety. The most commonly prescribed in this group would be temazepam, nitrazepam, lorazepam, and lormetazepam.

How do they work?

They work by boosting the level of a chemical transmitter in the brain called GABA. When this transmitter attaches to receptors on nerve cells in the brain, it reduces the level of electrical excitement in these cells, causing a feeling of calmness and, in high doses, sedation and then sleep.

Are there side effects?

The main side effect is drowsiness, which can carry over into the next day and make you feel quite groggy. They can also cause unsteadiness, problems with memory and concentration, and agitation.

They are also highly addictive, with around 40 per cent of people who take them every day for more than six weeks becoming inadvertently hooked. Symptoms of dependence are:

- cravings for them
- needing to take a higher dose to get the same effect
- feeling bad when you don't take them
- withdrawal symptoms when you stop them.

Drug treatments for insomnia **43**

These withdrawal symptoms can start pretty quickly for some people and usually within forty-eight hours. You might experience the following:

- insomnia
- agitation
- dizziness
- metallic taste
- blurred vision
- anxiety
- abdominal pains
- shortness of breath
- itching.

In fact, they can affect any part of your body and, in severe cases, even lead to fits. If you develop any of these symptoms of withdrawal, you will need to see your doctor, who can help treat them.

In general, they will only be given to you for a very short period if felt to be unavoidably necessary. They are not advisable if you are over sixty, pregnant, or breastfeeding, except as a last resort.

Z-drugs

As I've said, this group of drugs has this name because all its members' names begin with the letter "Z":

- zaleplon
- zolpidem
- zopiclone.

How do they work?

Although they have different chemical structures from the benzodiazepines, they work on the same receptors for the brain chemical GABA that we came across before. They were developed in the 1990s to try to overcome some of the problems associated with benzodiazepines, such as the groggy, hangover effect many people get the next morning.

They all have shorter half-lives (this is a scientific measure of the time it takes for your body to break down the drug to half its initial level in the bloodstream), which means they are in your system for much less time and so their effects wear off more quickly. The table below compares the half-lives of the Z-drugs and benzodiazepines.

Sleeping tablet	Half-life
Zaleplon	1 hour
Zolpidem	2–3 hours
Zopiclone	5 hours
Temazepam	8–9 hours
Lormetazepam	11 hours
Lorazepam	12–16 hours
Nitrazepam	29 hours

Are there any side effects?

Z-drugs have fewer side effects than benzodiazepines. The most common problems you might come across are:

• stomach upset

• drowsiness

• tingling skin

• difficulties with memory and concentration.

Drug treatments for insomnia

They are best avoided in pregnancy and breastfeeding, and should not be taken for more than four weeks because of the high risk of addiction. When you stop taking them, they can produce the same withdrawal effects as we've seen with benzodiazepines above.

If you have taken either of these groups of sleeping pills for more than four weeks or have withdrawal effects, you should see your doctor to discuss a detailed withdrawal programme that should help avoid unwanted symptoms and get you off them safely.

Other prescription medicines
Because of the unavoidable risk of addiction with the sleeping tablets we've looked at so far, your doctor may suggest that you try some other medicines which, although not originally designed for this purpose, do help you get to sleep.

Antidepressants
This group of pills has been found to be particularly useful. They will especially help if your poor sleep is due to low mood, stress, or anxiety, and they have the great advantage of not being addictive.

There are two main types of antidepressant used for this: the tricyclics (such as amitriptyline, dosulepin, and trazodone) and mirtazapine. They can both have a bit of a hangover effect the next day, when you may feel a bit dozy for an hour or two after waking, but this soon wears off for most people and can be minimized simply by taking the next night's dose an hour earlier.

As for side effects, these also wear off after a week or two but might include:

Tricyclics	Mirtazepine
Dry mouth	Constipation
Slightly blurred vision	Dry mouth
Becoming slower passing urine	Increased appetite
Constipation	Weight gain

Antihistamines

These anti-allergy tablets come in two varieties: drowsy and non-drowsy. And guess what? It's the drowsy ones that can be used to help sleep.

These can be bought directly from the pharmacy as proprietary brands, most notably Nytol, DreamOn, and Nightcalm (diphenhydramine). They can also be provided on prescription from your doctor as a non-addictive alternative to sleeping tablets.

Diphenhydramine is the most common of these, but you may also be given hydroxyzine or promethazine among others.

They are not suitable if you are pregnant or breastfeeding, or have liver disease or an eye condition called open angle glaucoma. Their side effects include: daytime sleepiness, headaches, dry mouth and blurring of vision. But they are not addictive and are generally well tolerated by most people.

Sleeping pills are harmless.

Although these medicines do have a place in the treatment
of insomnia for some people, their use should be severely
restricted. A large-scale study in the USA, published in the
BMJ Open journal in 2012, found an association between
taking as few as eighteen doses of sleeping pills per year
and increased risk of death. The phrase "dying to get a
good night's sleep" takes on a whole new meaning!

7
Alternative therapies

Given the addictive risk and possible side-effect profiles of prescription medicines used to treat sleep, you may want to try some of the complementary or alternative therapies that have been recommended to help insomnia. In this chapter we will take a look at a few of the most commonly suggested ones to see if they actually do work and if any of them can cause potentially harmful side effects. It's a common misconception that these therapies are all fluffy and lovely because they are "natural" and organic. Unfortunately, they can still have risks attached that are worth bearing in mind.

Acupuncture

What is it?
Acupuncture is a treatment that originated in ancient Chinese medicine. It looks at pain and illness in a way that suggests they are caused by imbalances in the body.

In particular, they are due to blockages in the flow of the body's energy called qi.

An acupuncturist will use a physical examination to assess your individual problem. They will then insert very fine needles into particular points on your body to release your energy and improve your symptoms.

How does it work?
It is believed to help both primary insomnia and secondary insomnia, particularly if triggered by pain or stress-related problems. It's thought that it works by stimulating nerves which cause the release of chemical messengers called neurotransmitters. In certain areas of the brain, these transmitters produce a calming, relaxing effect and can reduce pain.

Does it really work?
There is some research to suggest that it can directly help sleep, but this is not conclusive. There is no evidence to suggest harmful side effects, though.

Aromatherapy

What is it?
Aromatherapy is described by its proponents as the use of natural oils from the flowers, leaves, roots, and bark of various plants to promote physical and mental wellbeing. These so-called essential oils can be breathed in or rubbed onto the skin to achieve their effects.

Which oils are used to help sleep?
The two most recommended oils for insomnia are

chamomile and lavender. Other oils such as rosemary, grapefruit, lemon, and peppermint should be avoided, as they are too stimulating.

How do you use them?
There are a few ways in which these oils can be used:
- on a ball of cotton wool at the bedside
- a few drops in a warm bath before bed
- massaged directly into the skin
- bed linen spray.

Chamomile can also be drunk as a herbal tea.

Does it work?
Unfortunately, although there is some evidence to suggest that aromatherapy is relaxing and sleep-inducing, there's no proof as yet that it can actually treat insomnia. But there's no evidence it can do any harm, either. So even though it's definitely worth a try if you have trouble dropping off, don't expect miracles.

Melatonin

What is it?
Melatonin is a naturally occurring hormone found in many plants and animals. In humans, it is made in the pineal gland in the brain and is produced as part of the sleep–wake cycle, where it is responsible for causing sleepiness. The pineal gland is inactive during daylight hours but is switched on when the sun sets and it gets dark, and levels of melatonin go up. Because of this

natural effect in the body, a lot of people think that by taking it in pill form it will help with insomnia.

How do you take it?
Melatonin comes in straightforward tablet form but also in an orodispersible version which dissolves under your tongue. It is available without prescription from many pharmacies and health food shops, and you can also get it from your doctor.

Are there any side effects?
It can trigger a few side effects, most notably:

- headaches
- dizziness
- drowsiness
- irritability
- stomach upsets.

It is *not* safe in pregnancy or during breastfeeding.

Does it work?
Guess what! There's not enough evidence out there to be sure. However, it has been shown to help some people get off to sleep more quickly and to help with jet lag. It should not be used for more than thirteen weeks, though.

Valerian

What is it?
Valerian is a herbal supplement that comes from a perennial plant found throughout Europe and Asia. It

has been used as a medicine since the days of Ancient Greece and Rome, and both of the classical physicians Hippocrates and Galen mention its use, particularly as a sedative for treating sleeping problems.

How does it work?
The active ingredient is thought to be valeric acid, which works on the GABA receptors of brain cells that are the target of treatment with sleeping pills.

How do you take it?
It is available in tablet form, as an oil, and also as a tea you can drink.

Are there any side effects?
Unfortunately, any research done on treatment with valerian has only been carried out for twenty-eight days, so it's impossible to say whether it does any long-term harm. However, in the short term, other than headaches and, perhaps inevitably, drowsiness, it's largely free of side effects.

There's no reliable data about its use in pregnancy and breastfeeding, so most manufacturers say it should be avoided under these circumstances.

Does it work?
Some people swear by it, but officially there's no research evidence to support its use as a treatment for insomnia.

Herbal remedies or over-the-counter remedies are safer than drugs prescribed by the doctor.

Many herbal treatments have quite severe side effects and may not be safe if you are pregnant, breastfeeding, very young, or elderly. They can also interact with pills you are already taking. It is always best to check with your doctor or pharmacist before trying anything over the counter or from a herbalist.

8
Psychotherapy for insomnia

There are many different forms of psychotherapy that can help if you have secondary insomnia due to depression and anxiety. But the most useful and well-researched type of psychological therapy for primary insomnia is cognitive behavioural therapy (CBT).

In fact, we probably need to make more of a fanfare of this announcement, because CBT is by far the best, most effective, least harmful (zero harm and no side effects), most individualized of all the treatments for insomnia that are available (including pills and alternative remedies).

In short, if you can't sleep and your insomnia is really getting you down, then you'd be daft not to try CBT.

How does it work?
CBT works by helping to bring about a change in both the way you think about things (that's the cognitive bit)

and the way you act in response to those thoughts (the behavioural bit). It is a therapy that is only concerned with the here and now and does not go over things from your past that might be causing you to experience your current symptoms. It can also be used to help people with a wide range of other problems such as depression, anxiety, panic attacks, chronic pain, and obsessive compulsive disorder.

CBT for insomnia is brief, consisting of a limited number of sessions (usually ranging from six to eight) which use psychological and behaviour treatments alongside relaxation techniques and sleep hygiene education, in order to improve sleep.

The aim of CBT is to change factors in your life that encourage poor sleep to persist. Examples would include:

- cognitive factors such as worry, unhelpful or unrealistic beliefs and expectations about sleep

- behavioural factors, which could include any aspect of poor sleep hygiene

- physical factors such as mental and physical tension and hyper-arousal (see Chapter 3).

(Source: C. Morin and R. Benca, *The Lancet*, 2012)

What happens during CBT treatment for insomnia?

CBT has two components:

- The therapy sessions, during which your therapist will get to know you, discuss your problem, monitor your progress, and suggest ways to help you move forward when you get stuck.

- Homework between sessions, with the following exercises being commonly used to help you sleep better.

Sleep diary

The therapist will not only talk to you about your sleep difficulties to get a feel of your problem but will also obtain some objective evidence by asking you to fill out a detailed sleep diary. This will provide them with facts and figures about your insomnia which they can use to plan your treatment and monitor your progress.

Details in the log, which you will keep every day for around two weeks, will include the sort of information your doctor will have asked for if you consulted them first (see Chapter 4):

- time of last caffeinated drink before bed
- time of last alcohol before bed
- amount of exercise that day
- what time you went to bed
- when you turned off the light
- how long it took before you fell asleep
- how many times you woke during the night and for roughly how long
- what time you woke
- what time you got out of bed
- a rating of the quality of your sleep.

Stimulus control

The idea here is to encourage you to associate going to bed only with sleeping (or sex) and to stop you engaging in any other activities that are normally stimulating for your brain.

So the therapist will not only discuss good patterns of sleep hygiene with you (see Chapter 5) but will also encourage you specifically to:

- go to bed only when you are tired
- avoid watching television, going on the internet, or eating and drinking in bed
- get up and go to another room if you are still awake after half an hour.

Sleep restriction

Although it may seem a bit cruel to restrict the sleep of an insomniac even further, this therapy, which does just that, seems to work very well. You will be restricted to an amount of sleep each night that is based on what your sleep diary says is your usual. So a typical plan, using five hours as your limit, would involve the following:

- Going to bed at midnight and not before.
- No napping in the daytime.
- Setting an alarm to get up at five o'clock, no matter how badly you've slept.
- If you wake in the night or can't get off to sleep, stay in bed for fifteen minutes. If still no joy, get up, go to a different room, and return when you feel sleepy.
- As your sleep improves, your therapist will gradually increase the amount of time you are allowed to sleep in fifteen-minute weekly increments until you are able to go through the night.

This is as tough as it sounds for most people and will no doubt make you quite cranky to begin with. But if you stick with it, you will begin to get much better quality sleep and over time your body clock will be reset to a better pattern. It can take a few months for this to happen, though.

Relapse prevention

An important part of therapy is to encourage you to have a high level of vigilance for relapse of your insomnia. It's very easy to get back into bad habits quickly, so your therapist will teach you to start stimulus control again if things start to slip with your sleep and begin sleep restriction again if that doesn't work.

Does CBT work in primary insomnia?

It certainly does! Studies have found that 70–80 per cent of people who undergo this treatment find at least some improvement in their sleep, with 40 per cent reporting that they have been "cured".

On average, people treated with CBT find that they get to sleep about half an hour faster than previously and stay asleep for a further half an hour longer.

The really good news about this treatment, though, is that these beneficial effects are long-lasting. People who have been reviewed six months after treatment has ended continue to sleep much better.

Does CBT work in secondary insomnia?

Again, the answer is yes! People with a range of physical and mental health problems that can cause insomnia have had their sleep improved with the help of CBT. These include people with:

- depression
- fibromyalgia

- chronic pain
- cancer.

The improvements seen with both primary and secondary insomnia when treated with CBT are about the same.

Mythbuster

Sleep disorders are difficult to treat.
Thankfully, they can be treated, with the most effective remedies being good sleep hygiene and CBT. Neither of these works overnight, though, and if you want to shrug off your insomnia, you will have to put some effort in.

9
Shift work and jet lag

It used to be only New York that could be described as "the city that never sleeps", but in the twenty-first century there is not a corner of the developed world that doesn't have cities that are open for business around the clock. And long gone too are the days when only those carrying out essential services, such as emergency service workers, had to regularly work night shifts, and the few people out and about after midnight were those drunkenly waiting for taxis or the cab drivers themselves. Now you can visit supermarkets to do your weekly shop in the wee small hours, fill up your car with petrol, and then pick up some fast food on the way home. And of course you can shop online or chat with friends over the internet 24/7.

Not only that, but with air travel so much more easily available than it was even when I was a boy, there isn't a corner of the world that can't be reached in an aeroplane, which means we are much more likely to drag our bodies across time zones than ever before. In short, we are increasingly messing with our body clocks, and our sleep is suffering as a result.

Shift work

Shift work poses particular problems because it means we are exposed to light at times when our body clocks are expecting us to be in darkness. This applies not only if you work overnight and try to sleep during the day, but also if you work early shifts that mean you have to set an alarm to wake you before dawn. And given that it's thought that in industrialized countries around 20 per cent of us have these kinds of shift patterns, the associated sleep disturbances are very common.

Shift-work disorder

Fighting against your body clock to stay up at night and catch up with sleep in the daytime will invariably mean you are chronically sleep-deprived during the day and struggling to stay alert when you are at work. It will also mess up your hormone levels, your body temperature, and your digestive system, all of which function best when you are living with a regular day–night pattern. Not everyone who works shift patterns will be severely affected, but there's a high chance you may experience some symptoms.

How this can affect you

The most frequent symptoms of shift-work disorder are:

- insomnia
- sleepiness when you are awake

- headaches
- irritability
- being more accident-prone
- higher rates of sick leave.

What you can do to help

The trick is to make sleep your priority once you get home from a shift. So avoid distractions like TV, internet, and emails, and ask family and housemates to help you make a restful daytime environment.

Specific advice that can help includes:

- Have a relaxing bath before sleep.
- Don't do any vigorous exercise before going to bed.
- Buy some blackout curtains to keep the room dark.
- Make sure the room temperature is just right.
- Invest in ear plugs to block out noise, turn off your phone, and ask neighbours and family to keep external noise to a minimum.
- Don't go to bed hungry, so make sure you eat during your work shift but avoid heavy, fatty or spicy foods, and have fruit rather than chocolate as snacks.
- Avoid drinking caffeine too close to the end of your shift and drink plenty of water to stay well hydrated.
- Try to take short naps during breaks in your work.
- When coming off shifts, have a shorter sleep and then go to bed earlier that night.

Jet lag

Jet lag occurs when you travel long distances by air and arrive in a different time zone from the one you started in. The world is divided into twenty-four of these time zones and depending on which of these zones is facing the sun, it can be daytime on one part of the planet while it is simultaneously night on another. When it is midday in London, for example, it is 2 a.m. in Hawaii.

It is not the length of the flight that causes the problem but the distance travelled across time zones around the globe. The six-and-a-half-hour flight south from London to Freetown in Sierra Leone will not cause jet lag as both cities are in the same time zone, whereas the similar-length flight between New York and London across five time zones certainly will.

Symptoms of jet lag

Because jet lag has the same effect on your body clock as doing shift work, the symptoms are very similar. The severity of symptoms will depend on the number of time zones crossed, the time of day of departure and arrival, and the direction of travel (travelling east being worse than travelling west). Symptoms often include:

- insomnia
- irritability
- poor concentration
- tiredness
- indigestion

- upset bowel habit
- headaches.

Beating jet lag

It may take up to one day per time zone crossed to truly get over jet lag. There are, however, some tried and tested ways to minimize its effects and get through it without it ruining your trip too much.

- Start your journey feeling fresh, so get a good few nights' sleep before you fly.

- Factor in a stop-over on your journey if possible, as this will allow you to acclimatize to the time zone changes more gradually.

- Keep well hydrated by drinking plenty of water and soft drinks. Avoid alcohol and caffeine, which can both mess up your sleep pattern. If you are on a night flight, try to sleep as normal. Ear plugs and eye shades may help with this.

- Once you arrive, try to get at least four hours' sleep the first night in the new time zone. This is known as "anchor sleep" and will help you settle into your new routine.

- Try a warm bath before you go to bed at your destination to help you unwind.

- Avoid sleeping tablets and try the more natural methods listed above.

Travelling in first-class cabins on aeroplanes prevents jet lag.

Even though lying flat in a spacious cabin can certainly be more comfortable than trying to sleep upright in the busier economy section of a plane, you will cross the same number of time zones no matter how much you pay for your ticket, so you will be just as much at risk as those with cheaper seats.

10
Obstructive sleep apnoea

What is sleep apnoea?
The Greek word *apnoea* literally means "to stop breathing", and this is what happens to sufferers a varying number of times each night while they sleep. It's believed that in obstructive sleep apnoea (OSA) the muscles and soft tissues in the neck temporarily collapse during sleep, stopping air from getting into the trachea (windpipe). If the breathing stops for ten seconds or more each time, then it can be classified as true apnoea, and if there is only partial reduction of air intake of 50 per cent or more for ten seconds, then it is called hypopnoea.

What are the symptoms?
In OSA, the pauses in breathing are often noticed first by the person who shares a bed with the sufferer. They will often bring them to see a doctor because they have seen them stop breathing and are worried that one day they might not

start up again. As these pauses in breathing can happen as many as thirty times per hour in severe cases, that's a lot of episodes per night for a partner to worry about. People with OSA will often be loud snorers too, so their partners are likely to be awake to experience all of these apnoeas.

As well as stopping breathing at night, there are a number of other characteristic symptoms that will affect you during the day if you suffer from OSA. These include:

• feeling very sleepy and often dropping off very easily

• waking up with a sore or dry throat

• poor memory and concentration

• morning headaches

• irritability and restlessness

• mood disturbances such as anxiety and depression

• lack of interest in sex and possibly (in men) impotence

• raised blood pressure leading to an increased risk of heart disease and strokes.

What causes it?

As with many medical conditions, there is no single cause for OSA, and those things that put you at greater risk are what we refer to in the trade as "multifactorial". However, it will probably come as no surprise that three of them feature highly on every list of factors that contribute to most of our ill health – the unholy trinity: smoking, obesity, and alcohol.

Other causes include:

• being a man

• hitting middle age – OSA is most common in people over forty

- having a large neck and a double chin
- sleeping tablets and other medicines that cause sedation, such as antihistamines
- the menopause, which leads to relaxation of throat muscles because of hormone changes
- if OSA runs in the family
- diabetes
- nasal congestion.

How can it be diagnosed?

At the doctor's surgery

Your doctor will initially want to get a good history from you about your symptoms, preferably with collateral information from the person you share a bed, with as your partner will be the one who sees you stop breathing. The doctor will also carry out a routine physical examination of your heart, circulation, respiratory system, and throat and neck. They will also want to weigh you to get an idea of your body mass index (BMI) in order to check for obesity.

Alongside this, they are likely to either ask you to take away a questionnaire to bring back another time or go through it in your appointment. The questions are specifically about daytime symptoms in people with OSA and give a score on something called the Epworth Scale.

This scale was developed by an Australian doctor called Murray Johns in the early 1990s and is designed to look at daytime sleepiness caused by OSA. The answers given to the questions (see the box at the end of this chapter) produce a score that gives your doctor an idea of the degree of severity of symptoms you are having and therefore the likelihood that you have OSA.

Finally, they may request that you have a blood test for thyroid function, as an under-active thyroid gland will cause tiredness and can also be responsible for weight gain.

Once they have all your results, they will be able to tell you the likelihood that you have OSA or whether they think there's something else going on. If the results point towards OSA, then the next step will be a referral to a hospital sleep clinic for further investigation.

At the sleep clinic

The doctors and nurses at the clinic will go through your symptoms with you once more and review the results that your doctor will have sent on to them. They will then arrange for you to have a more detailed investigation of what happens when you are asleep, either by booking you to go into hospital overnight or by giving you the necessary equipment for a home assessment.

If you go into hospital you will have an investigation called polysomnography. This highfalutin term covers a number of painless and simultaneous procedures that the sleep clinic staff will be performing on you while you sleep in their unit. You will be wired up to all sorts of gadgets using electrodes, bands, and probes placed all over your head and body. These will be used to record your brainwaves, muscle tone, chest movements, heart rhythm, oxygen levels, nasal airflow, and the sound of your breathing and snoring.

Once the results have been analysed, you will be given a score of the severity of your symptoms so that appropriate treatment can be planned – more of which in a moment.

For home testing, you will be sent away from the clinic with a more basic version of the equipment that they use in hospital, which will also allow the sleep specialists to have readings of your oxygen levels and heart rate while you sleep, plus results from a breathing sensor, which will tell them how often you have apnoeas and for how long.

They will use this information to plan treatment, but they may still need to get you into hospital for polysomnography if the home test is inconclusive.

What treatment is there for OSA?

Lifestyle advice

As ever, there are quite a few things that you can do for yourself to improve your own symptoms. In the case of OSA, there is the infamous trio of:

- reducing alcohol intake
- losing weight
- stopping smoking.

In fact, if you do all these things, it will improve not only your sleep but your health in general. So why not give it a go!

Continuous positive airways pressure (CPAP)

You can't do this on your own as it requires the hospital to supply you with a fancy piece of equipment to take home and attach every night before sleep. And even though it may be a bit of a passion killer, it does work wonders for your sleep if you have moderate or severe OSA, and will make a big difference to how you feel in the daytime. It also improves blood pressure and risk of stroke by 40 per cent and risk of heart complications by 20 per cent – so good news all round.

The mask provides a constant flow of compressed air, which prevents the tissues of your throat from closing. It can feel odd at first but do stick with it as the effectiveness builds with time, and side effects such as nasal congestion, headaches, and flatulence will settle. Sleep clinic staff will also be happy to help you if you run into trouble with the apparatus.

Mandibular advancement splint

This simple device, which is like a very fancy version of the gum shields that rugby players wear, can help if you have only mild OSA or severe snoring. You put it into your mouth at night and during sleep it holds your jaw and tongue forward, which opens up your airway, making breathing easier and cutting down snoring.

You can buy them from various websites (see Appendix) and mould them yourself or – and this is probably best if you have had dental work such as bridges, caps, or crowns – your dental surgeon can make one for you.

Epworth Scale Questionnaire

How likely are you to doze off in the following daytime situations (as opposed to simply feeling tired)?

0   No chance
1   Slight chance
2   Moderate chance
3   High chance

Daytime Situations	Score
Sitting and reading	
Watching TV	
Sitting inactive in a public place (e.g. theatre or a meeting)	
As a passenger in a car for an hour without a break	
Lying down to rest in the afternoon when circumstances permit	
Sitting and talking to someone	
Sitting quietly after lunch without alcohol	
In a car, whilst stopped for a few minutes in traffic	

Once completed, this produces a score from 0 to 24. This then allows the doctor to calculate the severity of your symptoms.

0–10   Normal

10–12   Borderline

12–24   Severe

11
Sleep and teenagers

As the dad of two teenage boys, I am used to the sight of them lolloping down to weekend breakfast at midday and still being in their pyjamas at tea-time. As for school mornings, despite the fact that they are good at getting up with their alarms, they often look worse than I do (which, given my advance into middle age, takes some doing) as they search bleary-eyed for towels for the shower or bowls for their cereal, while making monosyllabic grunting sounds in response to my questions.

This is a massive change from their earlier years when they would be up, bright as buttons, at six o'clock sharp, chomping at the bit to play with their toys, do some painting, or, worse still, watch seemingly endless *Thomas the Tank Engine* videos. All of which meant that I or my wife had to drag ourselves from our warm bed and head downstairs to sit on the cold floor and play or watch TV with them.

But this change in their sleeping patterns – often viewed as slovenly, teenage laziness – actually comes from biological necessity. Adolescents genuinely need more sleep than both younger children and adults, and can suffer quite significantly if they don't get enough of it.

What is a normal sleeping pattern for teens?

Unlike younger children, who are often completely whacked out and sleepy by early evening, teenagers' body clocks often don't allow them to feel sleepy until around eleven o'clock at night. Once they have dropped off, they then need at least nine hours' sleep to ensure they are refreshed and alert the next day.

This explains why they are still on the go until late in the evening and why getting them up the next day can be a battle for parents and a trauma for them. However, in an age of social media and electronic games, many teenagers are now sabotaging their own chances of a good night's rest by Skypeing friends, updating their Facebook pages, Tweeting their followers, or playing online video games into the wee small hours. These activities keep their minds alert well beyond the eleven o'clock cut-off their brains are craving and cause further delay in sleep, long after they've switched off their electronic devices.

The sleep deprivation resulting from this can have a wide range of consequences, including:

- mood swings
- behavioural problems
- poor concentration
- daytime sleepiness, affecting school work
- increased risk of accidents (the biggest cause of death in teenagers)

- reduced immune system functioning, causing them to pick up frequent minor illnesses
- increased risk of obesity.

How can teenage sleep-related problems be prevented?

Much of the earlier advice regarding sleep hygiene for adults also holds for adolescents too.

- Work out a bedtime routine and stick to it. As we've seen, teens need nine hours' sleep from eleven o'clock, so work out a schedule that allows for this. This will include curbing the number of late nights out or evening working if they have a job.

- Reduce their intake of stimulant drinks, especially in the evenings. Energy drinks, coke, coffee, and tea will keep them awake at night, as will late-night snacking on sweets and chocolate bars.

- Encourage a period of winding down before bed. So no vigorous exercise like push-ups or sit-ups, maybe a relaxing bath or shower, and try to get them to settle down by reading rather than watching TV or catching up with their friends online.

- Installing a dimmer for their bedroom lights can also help set the mood for sleep. Dipping the lights as the evening goes on helps let their brains know that they need to start winding down for sleep.

- Have a designated time to unplug technology and social media devices. If this proves too problematic, then switching off the family wi-fi router at source will put a spanner in the works.

- Avoid encouraging the use of sleeping pills or any other medication; they aren't good for adults and should be avoided by teenagers at all costs.

Medical causes of sleep disturbances in teenagers

Sleep problems are a feature of a few medical conditions that can affect adolescents.

Narcolepsy

This condition, which usually begins during adolescence, has four classic symptoms:

- excessive daytime sleepiness (even dropping off while eating or talking)
- hypnagogic hallucinations (hallucinations as you drift into sleep or begin to wake up)
- cataplexy (sudden loss of muscle tone, which can lead to collapse)
- sleep paralysis (they are awake but unable to open their eyes for a few moments).

There are a number of specialist tests used to diagnose this and there are medications available to treat it. The first step to finding out if you or your teenager has narcolepsy would be to see your family doctor.

Obstructive sleep apnoea (OSA)

This can occur in adolescence and has the same symptoms we met in Chapter 10. Again, medical review is essential to make this diagnosis and access the right treatment.

Stress and depression

Emotional distress is a very common reason for sleep disruption. Short bouts of insomnia can be caused by worries about exams, break-ups with boyfriends and girlfriends, and, of course, bullying, be that at school or through social media.

Longer-term insomnia, however, can be due to true depression. This will feature other symptoms, including:

- poor appetite or overeating
- tearfulness
- moodiness and unusually aggressive behaviour
- isolation
- poor self-care
- self-harm
- suicidal thoughts and plans.

When poor sleep is accompanied by some or all of these symptoms, then it's very important to seek your doctor's advice, as your son or daughter may need counselling or other psychological support.

12
Restless legs syndrome and night cramps

Your legs can prove to be a particular nuisance when it comes to getting off to sleep, as they have two different tricks they can play on you when you get into bed, both of which are rare when you're awake and it wouldn't matter.

Restless legs syndrome

What is it?

The term "restless legs syndrome" was first coined in 1945 by Swedish medic Dr Karl Ekbom to describe a condition which produces weird, uncomfortable sensations in the legs at night which are only relieved by moving them.

It is a reasonably common neurological problem which affects up to 15 per cent of adults, is more common in women than men, and occurs more often as we get older.

What causes it?

It's not really known what causes it and most people are given the rather unsatisfactory diagnosis of idiopathic restless legs syndrome – which is a technical way of saying we haven't got a clue what's going on.

You might, however, have secondary restless legs syndrome, which means it is triggered by one of a wide range of other medical problems such as low iron, hypothyroidism, kidney disease, rheumatoid arthritis, fibromyalgia, diabetes, and Parkinson's disease. And it's also quite common in pregnancy, with one in five women suffering with it while they are expecting.

Some prescription medicines can also cause secondary restless legs syndrome as a side effect. These include antidepressants (such as amitriptyline, dosulepin, and fluoxetine), antihistamines, lithium, and some blood pressure tablets.

Other triggers are thought to include smoking, alcohol, caffeinated drinks, and being overweight – in fact, all the usual suspects that doctors like to warn you about.

Does it ever go away?

The good news is that if you have secondary restless legs syndrome, it will go away when the primary cause is treated, or not long after you've had your baby if you are pregnant.

If you have the idiopathic type of the problem, then I'm afraid there is no good news, as it is likely to get worse as you get older and very unlikely to go away on its own. If you develop it before you're forty-five, then this progression is likely to be slower than if you develop it later in life.

However, it's not all doom and gloom as there are a number of things that can be done to help your symptoms, and most people do get a significant amount of benefit, so they are well worth trying.

Self-help measures

A lot of the usual general health advice for sleeping better will help you avoid restless legs. So apologies if this list has a familiar ring to it, but there's no harm in being reminded of these things as they will help you get a better night's rest all round.

- Avoid stimulants in the evening such as caffeine and cigarettes.
- Lay off alcohol after your evening meal.
- Get some exercise during the daytime.
- Have a regular bedtime pattern and stick to it.

If you do still get restless legs, then it's worth giving the following measures a go as they can make an attack less severe:

- massaging the muscles of your legs
- putting a hot or cold compress on your leg muscles
- taking a warm bath before going to bed
- relaxation exercises
- leg stretches
- a cold shower
- reading a book as a distraction.

If this doesn't work, then it might be worth consulting your family doctor, as there are some prescription medicines that can help.

Medical treatments

There's no miracle cure available for restless legs, and unfortunately no two people will be guaranteed to react the same way to any pills, but there is a large amount of evidence to suggest that some of the drugs used to treat Parkinson's disease can be safe and effective for this condition.

The most commonly used of these medicines are:

- pramipexole

- ropinerole

- rotigotine.

It may be that the first one tried won't help, so don't be despondent if your doctor has to switch you to an alternative. You may also fall victim to the possible side effects of these treatments, which commonly include:

- drowsiness

- nausea

- dizziness

- headaches.

These can wear off once you get used to the medicine, so they are worth persevering with for a week or two before heading back to the doctor, unless, of course, they are severe, in which case you should stop straight away.

Other drugs that have been found to help are:

- painkillers such as codeine (although they can cause nausea and constipation and are potentially addictive)
- benzodiazepines such as clonazepam (again, these are highly addictive and so rarely used now).

Alternative medicine

Two herbal remedies that are often put forward as treatments for restless legs syndrome are:

- valerian
- St John's wort.

The evidence for their effectiveness is not very strong, however.

There's better evidence, though, for an osteopathic treatment called positional release manipulation (PRM), which involves holding parts of the body in certain positions to help reduce pain and discomfort. This would be available through a local osteopath.

Nocturnal leg cramps

These are very common, intense spasms in the muscles of the legs, which can be very painful and quite literally make your toes curl, or even make them stick up at ninety degrees from your foot. The muscles themselves will feel rock hard when they cramp up, and although the most commonly affected muscles are those in the calf and foot, they can affect any muscles right up to the thighs.

What causes them?

As with restless legs, the causes can be primary or secondary, with the most common primary cause once again being idiopathic.

Secondary causes include:

- injured, sprained, or overworked muscles
- dehydration or mineral imbalances such as low blood potassium
- medicines such as the contraceptive pill, statins for cholesterol, and some treatments for mental health conditions
- other medical problems including thyroid gland abnormalities, kidney problems, poor circulation (peripheral vascular disease), and multiple sclerosis
- pregnancy.

Self-help measures

There are a few self-help measures you can try in order to stop getting cramps and – surprise, surprise – the first of those is cutting down on alcohol and caffeine! Other suggestions include:

- Keep well hydrated by drinking plenty of fluids.
- Eat a range of foods that are rich in minerals like potassium, such as bananas, grapes, and tomatoes.
- Stretch your muscles every day.
- Don't go crazy when you exercise but always increase the amount you do gradually.
- Chat to your doctor if you think the cramps are caused by one of your prescription medicines.

If you still get cramps, then there are a few simple things that can sometimes stop them in their tracks:

- a hot flannel or compress placed on the affected muscles
- massaging the muscles
- getting out of bed and doing muscle stretches, or get a close friend to help (see below)

Medical treatments

If these simple things don't prevent your cramps or relieve them quickly when they occur, there are a couple of medicines that can be tried.

Over-the-counter painkillers such as paracetamol and ibuprofen can ease the symptoms, so it's worth having a chat with your local pharmacist before booking a doctor's appointment. If you do see your family doctor, they may suggest a trial of quinine tablets.

Quinine, which is mainly used as a treatment for the tropical disease malaria, can be very effective at treating night cramps, but it can have a few side effects that you need to look out for, so it will only be used as a last resort and with caution. Its common side effects include:

- nausea
- dizziness
- tinnitus (ringing in the ears)
- deafness
- visual disturbances
- nose bleeds and easy bruising.

If you try the drug and have these more serious side effects, you should let your doctor know straight away, as you will have to stop taking it:

- feeling very sleepy and often dropping off very easily
- waking up with a sore or dry throat
- poor memory and concentration
- morning headaches
- irritability and restlessness

- mood disturbances such as anxiety and depression
- lack of interest in sex and possibly (in men) impotence
- raised blood pressure leading to an increased risk of heart disease and strokes.

Appendix: Useful resources

The information in this book was gathered from a wide range of sources including books, scientific papers, and websites. I haven't referenced them in the text, in order to keep it uncluttered, but the following have been particularly helpful and are good sources of further information on the subject.

Books

Steven Lockley and Russell Foster, *Sleep: A Very Short Introduction*, Oxford: Oxford University Press, 2012. This short book is a very accessible introduction to the science of sleep. It looks in more detail at why we sleep, the biology of what happens while we are asleep, and some of the problems that can be caused by a lack of sleep.

Websites specifically about sleep

Canadian Sleep Society

This is the professional society in Canada for doctors and researchers who specialize in studying and treating the problems of sleep. Their website has a useful education section with evidence-based advice on all sleep problems.

http://www.canadiansleepsociety.ca

National Sleep Foundation
This American-based website features pages on good sleep hygiene, common sleep problems, and the science behind the sleep–wake cycle.

www.sleepfoundation.org

The Sleep Council
Although this organization was founded by British bed manufacturers, their website contains some good basic advice and surprisingly few advertisements.

www.sleepcouncil.org.uk/how-to-sleep

Sleep Health Foundation
This Australasian charity aims to raise awareness of sleep-related problems and their website offers advice to combat them.

www.sleephealthfoundation.org.au

General health websites with sleep advice
www.nhs.uk (UK National Health Service website)

www.patient.co.uk (website of evidence-based health advice)

www.netdoctor.co.uk (another excellent general health site)

www.rcpsych.orgac.uk (Royal College of Psychiatrists website, which has a section on insomnia)

www.mayoclinic.com (website of the Mayo Clinic in the USA, which features sleep problems)

Mandibular Advancement Splints
Aside from seeing your own dentist to discuss having a mould made for you, you can also purchase a mandibular advancement splint "off the peg", to mould yourself, from the following websites:

- britishsnoring.co.uk
- sleepguard.co.uk
- sleeppro.com

Also currently available in the "First Steps" series: